GOODSON MUMBA

THE ENGAGEMENT EQUATION

Balancing Employee Happiness and Customer Satisfaction

Copyright © 2024 by Goodson Mumba

All rights reserved. No part of this publication may be reproduced, stored or transmitted in any form or by any means, electronic, mechanical, photocopying, recording, scanning, or otherwise without written permission from the publisher. It is illegal to copy this book, post it to a website, or distribute it by any other means without permission.

First edition

ISBN: 9798335039475

This book was professionally typeset on Reedsy. Find out more at reedsy.com

Contents

Preface		iv
Acknowledgement		vi
Dedication		vii
Disclaimer		viii
1	Chapter One: The Discovery	1
2	Chapter Two: The Employee Perspective	6
3	Chapter Three: The Customer Perspective	12
4	Chapter Four: Finding the Balance	19
5	Chapter Five: Strategies for Employee Engagement	25
6	Chapter Six: Strategies for Customer Engagement	32
7	Chapter Seven: Measuring Engagement	39
8	Chapter Eight: Building a Culture of Engagement	47
9	Chapter Nine: Aligning Employee and Customer Engagement...	54
10	Chapter Ten: Overcoming Challenges	60
11	Chapter Eleven: Case Studies: Best Practices	67
12	Chapter Twelve: Future Trends in Engagement	75
13	Chapter Thirteen: Ethical Considerations	81
14	Chapter Fourteen: Global Perspectives on Engagement	88
15	Chapter Fifteen: The Engagement Equation in Action	94
About the Author		101

Preface

In today's rapidly evolving business landscape, organizations face an ever-increasing challenge: how to balance the twin pillars of employee happiness and customer satisfaction. These two elements, often treated separately, are inextricably linked. When employees are engaged and fulfilled, they are more likely to deliver exceptional service, fostering a positive experience for customers. Conversely, satisfied customers can invigorate and inspire the workforce, creating a virtuous cycle of engagement and success.

"The Engagement Equation: Balancing Employee Happiness and Customer Satisfaction" explores this critical dynamic, offering insights and strategies for leaders, managers, and teams who seek to create a thriving organizational environment. Through practical guidance, real-world examples, and thoughtful analysis, this book aims to provide a comprehensive roadmap for aligning employee and customer engagement strategies.

Our journey begins with an exploration of the fundamentals of engagement, setting the stage for a deeper understanding of its impact on performance and satisfaction. We then delve into the perspectives of both employees and customers, examining the motivations, needs, and expectations that drive their engagement. By understanding these key drivers, we can develop strategies that resonate with both groups, fostering a culture of mutual respect and collaboration.

The heart of this book lies in the integration of employee and customer engagement strategies. We explore the power of cross-functional collaboration, breaking down silos to create cohesive and aligned efforts. We also highlight the importance of co-creation, engaging customers in the product development process to drive innovation and relevance. By aligning these strategies, organizations can create a seamless and harmonious experience for all stakeholders.

In the final chapters, we address the practical aspects of implementing engagement strategies, from developing an engagement roadmap to measuring progress and adjusting approaches. We also look to the future, exploring emerging trends and technologies that will shape the landscape of engagement in the years to come.

"The Engagement Equation" is more than just a book; it is a call to action. It challenges us to rethink our approach to engagement, recognizing the profound impact it has on both employees and customers. It encourages us to embrace a holistic and integrated perspective, where the happiness of employees and the satisfaction of customers are not mutually exclusive but mutually reinforcing.

As you embark on this journey, I hope you find inspiration, practical advice, and a renewed sense of purpose. Together, we can create organizations where employees and customers thrive, driving sustained success and making a positive difference in the world.

Welcome to "The Engagement Equation."

Sincerely,

Goodson Mumba

Acknowledgement

I would like to eternally and gratefully acknowledge the Almighty God for the infinite intelligence from His universal mind where we draw from all that we come to know and are yet to know. May I also acknowledge and thank everyone that has played a part in my journey of life in terms of spiritual, moral, emotional and material support.

Dedication

I extend my sincerest gratitude to my beloved wife, Edith Mumba, and our children, Angelina, Lubuto, Letticia, Lulumbi, and Butusho, for their unwavering support and understanding throughout the conception, writing, and eventual publication of this book, despite the sacrifices and challenges they endured.

Disclaimer

This book is a work of fiction. Names, characters, businesses, places, events, and incidents are either the products of the author's imagination or used in a fictitious manner. Any resemblance to actual persons, living or dead, or actual events is purely coincidental.

1

Chapter One: The Discovery

In the heart of the bustling city, amidst the towering buildings, Angela, the dedicated HR manager of BrightWorks Inc., sat in her office, her brow furrowed with concern. The once vibrant atmosphere of the company seemed to be fading, overshadowed by the looming specter of high employee turnover and slipping customer satisfaction scores.

As Angela poured over the latest data, her heart sank. The numbers painted a bleak picture - disengaged employees, a lack of motivation, and dissatisfied customers. It was a puzzle she was determined to solve.

With resolve burning in her eyes, Angela rose from her desk and made her way through the maze of cubicles, determined to uncover the root of the problem. She listened intently as employees shared their frustrations, their voices tinged with disappointment and disillusionment.

Angela's footsteps echoed down the corridors as she ventured deeper into the heart of the company, seeking answers among the ranks of her colleagues. She witnessed the fatigue etched on their faces, the passion dimmed by monotony and routine.

But amidst the despair, Angela glimpsed flickers of hope - employees who still believed in the company's mission, who longed to be valued and heard. Their stories resonated with her, igniting a fire within her soul.

Returning to her office, Angela sat in silence, her mind racing with possibilities. She knew that understanding engagement was the key to unlocking BrightWorks' potential. It was not just about numbers on a spreadsheet; it was about the people - their dreams, their struggles, their aspirations.

With newfound determination, Angela set out to redefine engagement, to breathe life back into the company's culture. For Angela, the journey had only just begun, but she was ready to face the challenges head-on. The engagement imperative was clear - it was time to balance employee happiness and customer satisfaction, no matter the cost.

Defining Engagement

Angela sat at her desk, her mind buzzing with thoughts and ideas. She realized that before she could tackle the challenges ahead, she needed to define what engagement truly meant for BrightWorks Inc. With determination in her heart, she began to unravel the complex web of employee and customer engagement.

Employee Engagement

In her quest to define engagement, Angela turned her focus to the heartbeat of the company - its employees. She conducted interviews, held focus groups, and poured over surveys, seeking to understand what motivated and inspired her colleagues.

As she listened to their stories, Angela discovered that engagement went beyond mere job satisfaction. It was about a sense of purpose, a feeling of belonging, and a connection to the company's mission. It was about employees feeling valued, respected, and empowered to make a difference.

With this newfound understanding, Angela crafted a definition of employee engagement that resonated with the soul of BrightWorks Inc. It was a commitment to fostering a culture of trust, collaboration, and growth - a culture where every employee felt invested in the company's success.

Customer Engagement

But Angela knew that engagement did not end with the employees; it extended to the company's loyal customers as well. With this in mind, she turned her attention to understanding what drove customer engagement.

Through in-depth market research and customer feedback, Angela uncovered the intricacies of customer engagement. She learned that it was more than just satisfaction with a product or service; it was about building meaningful relationships, delivering exceptional experiences, and creating brand advocates.

Armed with this knowledge, Angela crafted a definition of customer engagement that captured the essence of BrightWorks Inc.'s relationship with its clientele. It was a commitment to exceeding expectations, listening to feedback, and continuously innovating to meet the evolving needs of customers.

As the day drew to a close, Angela sat back in her chair, a sense of accomplishment washing over her. She had taken the first step on her journey to balance employee happiness and customer satisfaction. With a clear understanding of engagement in hand, she was ready to forge ahead, determined to lead BrightWorks Inc. to a brighter future.

Importance of Engagement

As Angela delved deeper into her exploration of engagement, she realized the critical importance it held for BrightWorks Inc. She understood that engagement was not just a lofty ideal but a fundamental driver of company performance and customer satisfaction.

Impact on Performance

With a furrowed brow, Angela pored over the company's performance metrics, her eyes scanning the rows of data with keen interest. She noticed a clear pattern emerging - departments with higher levels of employee engagement consistently outperformed their counterparts.

Angela saw that engaged employees were more productive, more creative, and more committed to achieving the company's goals. Their passion and enthusiasm permeated every aspect of their work, driving innovation and excellence across the organization.

As she analyzed the numbers, Angela realized the profound impact that engagement had on BrightWorks' bottom line. Engaged employees were not just assets; they were the lifeblood of the company, fueling its growth and success.

CHAPTER ONE: THE DISCOVERY

Relationship to Satisfaction

But Angela knew that engagement was not just about performance; it was also intricately linked to customer satisfaction. She understood that engaged employees were more likely to deliver exceptional service, going above and beyond to meet the needs of their customers.

Angela saw firsthand how engaged employees fostered stronger relationships with customers, building trust and loyalty that transcended transactions. Their genuine care and dedication shone through in every interaction, leaving a lasting impression on the company's clientele.

As she reflected on the connection between employee engagement and customer satisfaction, Angela realized that they were two sides of the same coin. Engaged employees were the driving force behind satisfied customers, creating a virtuous cycle of success for BrightWorks Inc.

With this newfound insight, Angela felt a renewed sense of purpose. She knew that by prioritizing engagement, she could not only improve company performance but also elevate the customer experience. The importance of engagement was clear - it was the key to unlocking BrightWorks' full potential and achieving lasting success.

2

Chapter Two: The Employee Perspective

In the bustling corridors of BrightWorks Inc., Angela embarked on a journey to uncover the true heartbeat of the company - its employees. Armed with a notepad and a genuine curiosity, she set out to understand their perspective, their hopes, their dreams, and their frustrations.

As she walked through the open office space, Angela observed the flurry of activity around her. Yet, beneath the surface, she sensed a quiet discontent lingering in the air. It was a feeling she knew all too well - the subtle signs of disengagement that threatened to erode the company's morale.

With determination in her heart, Angela approached her first interviewee - Sarah, a seasoned software developer known for her expertise and dedication. As they sat down together in a cozy corner of the office, Angela listened intently as Sarah poured out her heart.

Sarah spoke of her love for coding, her passion for problem-solving, and her desire to make a meaningful impact through her work. Yet, amidst the chaos of deadlines and project pressures, she felt increasingly disconnected from the company's mission. She longed for more recognition, more autonomy, more opportunities to grow and develop her skills.

Angela nodded empathetically, taking note of Sarah's concerns. She knew that Sarah's experience was not unique - it echoed the sentiments of many employees across the company. They craved more than just a paycheck; they yearned for a sense of purpose, a sense of belonging, a sense of fulfillment.

With each conversation, Angela gained deeper insights into the lives of her colleagues. She heard stories of triumph and tribulation, of joy and frustration, of dreams deferred and aspirations unfulfilled. Yet, amidst the challenges, she also glimpsed flickers of hope - employees who still believed in the company's potential, who remained committed to making a difference, who yearned for a leader to guide them forward.

As the day drew to a close, Angela reflected on the richness of her interactions. She realized that the employee perspective was not just a collection of voices; it was the soul of the company, the driving force behind its success. And with each story she heard, Angela felt more determined than ever to champion the cause of employee engagement, to create a workplace where every individual felt valued, respected, and empowered to thrive.

With a renewed sense of purpose, Angela set out to translate her insights into action. She knew that the journey ahead would be challenging, but she was ready to face it head-on. For Angela, the employee perspective was not just a chapter in a book; it was the foundation upon which BrightWorks Inc. would build a brighter future.

Motivation and Morale

As Angela delved deeper into her exploration of the employee perspective, she found herself grappling with the complex dynamics of motivation and morale. She understood that the key to unlocking employee engagement lay in understanding the factors that drove individuals to excel in their roles.

Intrinsic vs. Extrinsic Motivation

Angela sat down with Mark, a talented graphic designer known for his creative flair and attention to detail. As they sipped coffee in the company break room, Angela probed into what fueled Mark's passion for design.

Mark spoke passionately about his love for art and his desire to express himself through his work. He described the joy he felt when he brought his ideas to life on the canvas, the sense of fulfillment that came from creating something truly unique.

But amidst the praise and recognition, Mark also revealed a deeper truth - the struggle to maintain his creative spark in the face of external pressures and deadlines. He spoke of the constant battle between his intrinsic motivation - the desire to create for the sheer joy of it - and the extrinsic rewards of praise and recognition.

Angela listened intently, empathizing with Mark's plight. She understood that true engagement could not be achieved through external incentives alone; it required tapping into the intrinsic motivations that drove individuals to excel.

CHAPTER TWO: THE EMPLOYEE PERSPECTIVE

Creating a Positive Work Environment

With Mark's words echoing in her mind, Angela set out to create a more positive work environment at BrightWorks Inc. She knew that fostering a culture of appreciation, support, and collaboration was essential to boosting morale and motivating employees to do their best work.

Angela worked closely with department heads to implement initiatives aimed at recognizing and celebrating employee achievements. From monthly awards ceremonies to team-building activities, Angela sought to create opportunities for employees to connect, collaborate, and celebrate their successes together.

She also focused on enhancing the physical workspace, transforming dull cubicles into vibrant, creative hubs where employees felt inspired and energized to tackle their tasks. With the addition of plants, artwork, and comfortable seating areas, Angela hoped to create an environment where creativity could flourish and morale could soar.

As the days passed, Angela noticed a subtle shift in the atmosphere at BrightWorks Inc. Employees seemed more engaged, more enthusiastic, more invested in the company's success. Morale was on the rise, and with it, so too was the potential for greatness.

With each small victory, Angela felt a renewed sense of optimism. She knew that the journey to foster motivation and morale was far from over, but she was determined to continue pushing forward. For Angela, creating a positive work environment wasn't just a goal - it was a commitment to nurturing the potential of every individual at BrightWorks Inc.

Leadership and Communication

As Angela delved deeper into her exploration of the employee perspective, she recognized the pivotal role that leadership and communication played in fostering engagement within the company. She understood that effective leadership and open communication were the cornerstones of a thriving workplace culture.

Role of Leadership in Engagement

Angela sat down with David, a seasoned team leader known for his charismatic leadership style and ability to inspire those around him. As they conversed in David's corner office, Angela probed into his approach to leading his team.

David spoke passionately about his belief in the power of servant leadership - a leadership style focused on empowering and supporting team members to achieve their full potential. He described the importance of leading by example, of fostering trust and transparency, and of creating a culture of accountability and ownership.

But amidst the praise for David's leadership, Angela also unearthed a deeper truth - the impact that ineffective leadership could have on employee engagement. She heard stories of micromanagement, lack of direction, and a disconnect between leadership and frontline employees.

With David's insights fresh in her mind, Angela recognized the critical importance of cultivating strong leadership within BrightWorks Inc. She knew that the key to unlocking employee engagement lay in empowering leaders at all levels to lead with empathy, integrity, and vision.

CHAPTER TWO: THE EMPLOYEE PERSPECTIVE

Effective Communication Strategies

Armed with a newfound understanding of the role of leadership in engagement, Angela turned her attention to the importance of effective communication within the company. She understood that clear, transparent communication was essential to building trust, fostering collaboration, and aligning employees with the company's goals.

Angela worked closely with the company's communication team to develop strategies aimed at improving communication channels and processes. From regular town hall meetings to open-door policies, Angela sought to create opportunities for employees to voice their concerns, share their ideas, and connect with leadership on a personal level.

She also emphasized the importance of listening - truly listening - to the needs and feedback of employees. Through surveys, feedback sessions, and one-on-one conversations, Angela sought to gain insights into the challenges and aspirations of her colleagues, ensuring that their voices were heard and valued.

As the days turned into weeks, Angela witnessed a transformation within BrightWorks Inc. Employees felt more connected, more engaged, more inspired to contribute their best work. Leadership was more visible, more accessible, more attuned to the needs of their teams. And communication flowed freely, fostering a culture of transparency and trust.

With each passing day, Angela felt a renewed sense of optimism. She knew that the journey to foster engagement was far from over, but she was confident that with strong leadership and effective communication, BrightWorks Inc. would continue to thrive and succeed.

3

Chapter Three: The Customer Perspective

In the heart of BrightWorks Inc., Angela turned her attention to understanding the company's customers - the lifeblood of its success. With a determination to uncover the true essence of customer engagement, she embarked on a journey to explore their needs, desires, and expectations.

As Angela sifted through piles of customer feedback and survey data, she realized that the customer perspective was as diverse as the individuals themselves. Each interaction, each experience, held valuable insights into the intricate relationship between BrightWorks Inc. and its clientele.

With a stack of customer profiles in hand, Angela set out to immerse herself in the world of the company's most loyal patrons. From busy executives to tech-savvy millennials, she sought to understand what drove their loyalty, what delighted them, and what left them wanting more.

Angela's first stop was a coffee shop downtown, where she met with Lisa, a longtime customer and avid supporter of BrightWorks Inc.'s products. As they sipped their lattes,

CHAPTER THREE: THE CUSTOMER PERSPECTIVE

Angela listened intently as Lisa shared her experiences with the company.

Lisa spoke of the seamless experience she had when purchasing her latest gadget, the personalized service she received from the customer support team, and the sense of belonging she felt as part of the BrightWorks Inc. community. But amidst the praise, Lisa also voiced her concerns - the occasional product glitches, the lack of customization options, the need for more responsive communication channels.

With Lisa's insights in mind, Angela delved deeper into the world of customer experience, seeking to uncover the moments of truth that shaped their perceptions of BrightWorks Inc. From initial contact to post-purchase support, she mapped out the customer journey, identifying pain points and opportunities for improvement.

Armed with a clearer understanding of the customer perspective, Angela set out to implement initiatives aimed at enhancing the customer experience. From streamlining the ordering process to offering personalized recommendations, she sought to delight customers at every touch point, leaving a lasting impression that would keep them coming back for more.

As the days turned into weeks, Angela witnessed a transformation within BrightWorks Inc. Customers felt more valued, more appreciated, more connected to the company and its products. Their loyalty grew stronger, their satisfaction scores soared, and with each interaction, the bond between BrightWorks Inc. and its customers deepened.

With a sense of satisfaction and accomplishment, Angela knew that the journey to understand the customer perspective was far from over. But armed with insights and empathy, she was ready to continue shaping BrightWorks Inc. into a company that not only met but exceeded the expectations of its most important stakeholders - its customers.

Customer Experience

With a stack of customer profiles in hand, Angela delved deeper into the world of customer experience, determined to uncover the key moments that shaped their interactions with BrightWorks Inc. She knew that understanding the customer journey was essential to crafting meaningful experiences that would delight and engage customers at every touch point.

Journey Mapping

Armed with markers and a blank canvas, Angela set out to map the intricate journey that customers embarked upon when interacting with BrightWorks Inc. From the initial discovery phase to post-purchase support, she meticulously charted each step, seeking to understand the highs and lows that defined the customer experience.

As she traced the customer journey, Angela uncovered a series of touchpoints - some smooth and seamless, others fraught with frustration and confusion. She identified areas where customers encountered roadblocks, where their needs were unmet, and where opportunities for improvement lay hidden beneath the surface.

With each stroke of her pen, Angela gained deeper insights into the customer perspective. She saw the world through their eyes, felt the highs of success and the lows of disappointment, and recognized the importance of delivering a consistent and cohesive experience that would resonate with customers at every stage of their journey.

Moments of Truth

But amidst the complexity of the customer journey, Angela also unearthed moments of truth - those pivotal encounters that had the power to shape the customer's perception of BrightWorks Inc. These were the moments when the company's true character was revealed, when its commitment to excellence and customer satisfaction was put to the test.

Angela listened intently as customers recounted their experiences - the first impression they received when visiting the company's website, the support they received when reaching out to customer service, the joy they felt when unboxing their latest purchase. But she also heard stories of frustration - the long wait times, the confusing navigation, the lack of personalized recommendations.

With each moment of truth, Angela recognized the opportunity to make a difference. She saw the chance to turn a negative experience into a positive one, to surprise and delight customers with unexpected acts of kindness and generosity, to build trust and loyalty that would endure long into the future.

Armed with her newfound understanding of the customer experience, Angela set out to implement initiatives aimed at enhancing every touch point along the customer journey. From redesigning the website to streamlining the checkout process, she sought to create a seamless and enjoyable experience that would leave customers feeling valued, appreciated, and eager to return.

As the days turned into weeks, Angela witnessed a transformation within BrightWorks Inc. Customers felt more connected, more engaged, more loyal to the company and its products. With each interaction, they experienced moments of truth that reinforced their belief in BrightWorks Inc.'s commitment to excellence and customer satisfaction.

With a sense of pride and accomplishment, Angela knew that the journey to understand the customer perspective was far from over. But armed with insights and empathy, she was ready to continue shaping BrightWorks Inc. into a company that not only met but exceeded the expectations of its most important stakeholders - its customers.

Customer Satisfaction

As Angela delved deeper into the world of customer experience, she recognized that the ultimate goal was to not only meet but exceed customer satisfaction. She understood that by truly understanding customer needs and delivering exceptional service, BrightWorks Inc. could create a loyal and enthusiastic customer base that would propel the company to success.

Understanding Customer Needs

Armed with a newfound appreciation for the importance of customer satisfaction, Angela set out to gain a deeper understanding of the needs, desires, and aspirations of BrightWorks Inc.'s clientele. She knew that by listening intently to their feedback and insights, she could uncover valuable opportunities to enhance the customer experience.

Angela embarked on a series of one-on-one interviews and focus groups with customers from all walks of life. From tech enthusiasts to business professionals, she sought to uncover the unique challenges and pain points they faced in their interactions with BrightWorks Inc.

As she listened to their stories, Angela gained valuable insights into the diverse needs and preferences of the company's clientele. She heard tales of frustration with outdated technology, confusion over complex product features, and disappointment with inconsistent customer service.

But amidst the challenges, Angela also unearthed opportunities - opportunities to innovate, to evolve, to create products and services that truly met the needs of customers. Armed with this newfound knowledge, she set out to implement initiatives aimed at addressing customer pain points and exceeding their expectations.

Delivering Exceptional Service

But Angela knew that understanding customer needs was only half the battle; the true measure of success lay in delivering exceptional service that went above and beyond. With this in mind, she worked closely with the customer service team to implement strategies aimed at delighting customers at every touch point.

From personalized greetings to proactive problem-solving, Angela sought to create a customer service experience that was as seamless and enjoyable as possible. She trained her team to anticipate customer needs, to empathize with their concerns, and to go the extra mile to ensure their satisfaction.

As the days turned into weeks, Angela witnessed a transformation within BrightWorks Inc. Customers felt more valued, more appreciated, more connected to the company and its products. With each interaction, they experienced moments of delight that reinforced their loyalty and commitment to the brand.

With a sense of pride and accomplishment, Angela knew that the journey to exceed customer satisfaction was far from over. But armed with insights and empathy, she was ready to continue shaping BrightWorks Inc. into a company that not only met but exceeded the expectations of its most important stakeholders - its customers.

4

Chapter Four: Finding the Balance

As Angela continued her journey to enhance employee happiness and customer satisfaction at BrightWorks Inc., she realized that the key to success lay in finding the delicate balance between the two. With determination in her heart, she set out to navigate the complexities of aligning the needs of employees with the expectations of customers.

In her quest to find the balance, Angela convened a series of meetings with key stakeholders from across the company - from department heads to frontline employees to loyal customers. Together, they embarked on a journey of discovery, seeking to understand the interconnectedness of employee engagement and customer satisfaction.

As they brainstormed ideas and shared insights, Angela realized that finding the balance required more than just strategic planning; it demanded a fundamental shift in mindset. It was about recognizing that happy employees led to satisfied customers and vice versa - that the two were intrinsically linked in a symbiotic relationship.

Armed with this newfound understanding, Angela set out to

implement initiatives that would foster a culture of engagement within BrightWorks Inc. From employee recognition programs to customer appreciation events, she sought to create opportunities for employees and customers alike to feel valued and appreciated.

But amidst the excitement of implementing new initiatives, Angela faced challenges along the way. She encountered resistance from some employees who were hesitant to embrace change, and skepticism from customers who were wary of unfamiliar approaches.

Yet, Angela remained undeterred. She knew that finding the balance was not a one-time endeavor but an ongoing process of adaptation and evolution. With patience and perseverance, she continued to refine her approach, learning from both successes and setbacks along the way.

As the days turned into weeks and the weeks into months, Angela began to see the fruits of her labor. Employee morale improved, customer satisfaction scores soared, and a sense of harmony permeated throughout BrightWorks Inc.

With a sense of pride and accomplishment, Angela knew that she had achieved her goal of finding the balance between employee happiness and customer satisfaction. But she also recognized that the journey was far from over. As the company continued to grow and evolve, so too would the need to continually strive for balance in all aspects of its operations. And with Angela leading the way, BrightWorks Inc. was poised to achieve even greater heights of success in the years to come.

CHAPTER FOUR: FINDING THE BALANCE

Aligning Goals and Values

As Angela delved deeper into her quest to find the balance between employee happiness and customer satisfaction, she realized that aligning the goals and values of BrightWorks Inc. was essential to achieving this delicate equilibrium. With determination in her heart, she set out to ensure that the company's mission and vision were in harmony with the shared values of both employees and customers.

Mission and Vision Alignment

Angela convened a meeting with the company's leadership team to discuss the alignment of BrightWorks Inc.'s mission and vision with the needs and expectations of its employees and customers. Together, they revisited the company's core values, its guiding principles, and its long-term aspirations.

As they deliberated, Angela recognized the importance of crafting a mission and vision statement that resonated with the soul of the company - a statement that captured the essence of what BrightWorks Inc. stood for and where it was headed in the future.

After much discussion and debate, they arrived at a consensus - a mission to empower individuals and organizations to achieve their full potential through innovative technology solutions, and a vision to be the leading provider of cutting-edge products and services that enhance the lives of customers around the world.

Shared Values between Employees and Customers

But Angela knew that a mission and vision were only as powerful as the values that underpinned them. With this in mind, she set out to identify the shared values that united employees and customers in their journey with BrightWorks Inc.

Through surveys, focus groups, and one-on-one interviews, Angela uncovered a common thread that bound them together - a commitment to excellence, integrity, and collaboration. From employees who took pride in their work to customers who valued honesty and transparency, the shared values of BrightWorks Inc. ran deep within its DNA.

With these shared values in mind, Angela set out to foster a culture of alignment within the company. She worked closely with department heads to integrate the company's values into every aspect of its operations - from hiring and onboarding to product development and customer service.

As the days turned into weeks, Angela witnessed a transformation within BrightWorks Inc. Employees felt more connected, more aligned with the company's mission and vision. Customers, too, felt a deeper sense of trust and loyalty towards the brand, knowing that their values were reflected in every interaction.

With a sense of pride and accomplishment, Angela knew that she had achieved her goal of aligning the goals and values of BrightWorks Inc. But she also recognized that the journey was far from over. As the company continued to grow and evolve, so too would the need to continually reaffirm its commitment to excellence, integrity, and collaboration. And with Angela leading the way, BrightWorks Inc. was poised to achieve even greater heights of success in the years to come.

Managing Expectations

As Angela navigated the intricate landscape of aligning goals and values at BrightWorks Inc., she recognized the importance of managing expectations - both internally among employees and externally with customers. With determination in her heart, she set out to set realistic expectations and overcome challenges along the way.

Setting Realistic Expectations

Angela gathered her team together for a strategy session, emphasizing the importance of setting realistic expectations for both employees and customers. She knew that by establishing clear goals and timelines, they could ensure alignment and avoid disappointment down the line.

Together, they outlined a roadmap for the company's future, setting achievable targets for employee engagement and customer satisfaction. They communicated these expectations openly and transparently, ensuring that everyone understood their role in the journey ahead.

As they finalized their plan, Angela felt a sense of confidence knowing that they were setting the stage for success. By managing expectations effectively, they could pave the way for a smoother and more harmonious transition towards achieving their goals.

Overcoming Challenges

But Angela knew that managing expectations was easier said than done, especially in the face of unforeseen challenges and obstacles. As they embarked on their journey, they encountered resistance from some employees who were hesitant to embrace change and skepticism from customers who were wary of unfamiliar approaches.

Yet, Angela remained undeterred. She knew that challenges were an inevitable part of the journey towards finding the balance between employee happiness and customer satisfaction. With resilience and determination, she led her team forward, confronting each obstacle head-on and turning setbacks into opportunities for growth and learning.

Through perseverance and creativity, they found innovative solutions to overcome challenges, whether it was implementing new training programs to address employee concerns or launching targeted marketing campaigns to win over skeptical customers.

As the days turned into weeks and the weeks into months, Angela witnessed a transformation within BrightWorks Inc. Despite the challenges they faced, they emerged stronger and more united than ever before. By managing expectations effectively and overcoming obstacles together, they had laid the foundation for a brighter future filled with endless possibilities.

With a sense of pride and accomplishment, Angela knew that the journey to finding the balance was far from over. But armed with the lessons learned and the bonds forged along the way, BrightWorks Inc. was ready to face whatever challenges lay ahead and continue their quest towards achieving true harmony between employee happiness and customer satisfaction.

5

Chapter Five: Strategies for Employee Engagement

As Angela delved deeper into her mission to foster employee happiness and satisfaction at BrightWorks Inc., she knew that implementing effective strategies for employee engagement was essential. With a sense of purpose, she embarked on a journey to explore innovative approaches to empower and inspire her colleagues.

Angela convened a meeting with the HR team, eager to brainstorm ideas and develop a comprehensive plan for enhancing employee engagement. Together, they poured over research, analyzed best practices, and drew upon their own experiences to craft a series of strategies aimed at creating a vibrant and dynamic workplace culture.

1. **Building a Culture of Recognition**: Angela recognized the power of appreciation in boosting morale and motivation among employees. They developed a system for recognizing and celebrating individual and team achievements, whether it was through employee of the month

awards, peer-to-peer recognition programs, or public acknowledgments during company meetings.

2. **Encouraging Professional Development**: Angela understood the importance of investing in the growth and development of her colleagues. They launched a variety of professional development initiatives, including mentorship programs, skills training workshops, and tuition reimbursement opportunities, empowering employees to expand their skill sets and advance their careers.

3. **Promoting Work-Life Balance**: Angela recognized the need to support employees in achieving a healthy balance between their professional and personal lives. They implemented flexible work arrangements, wellness programs, and initiatives to promote mental health and wellbeing, ensuring that employees felt valued and supported both in and out of the workplace.

4. **Fostering Open Communication**: Angela believed that fostering a culture of open communication was essential to building trust and transparency within the organization. They implemented regular feedback sessions, anonymous suggestion boxes, and town hall meetings, providing opportunities for employees to voice their concerns, share their ideas, and connect with leadership on a personal level.

5. **Creating Opportunities for Collaboration**: Angela understood the power of collaboration in driving innovation and creativity within the company. They facilitated cross-departmental projects, team-building activities, and social events, fostering a sense of camaraderie and teamwork among employees and encouraging them to share ideas and work together towards common goals.

As the days passed, Angela witnessed a transformation within BrightWorks Inc. Employees felt more engaged, more motivated, and more connected to the company's mission and vision. With each strategy they implemented, they moved one step closer towards creating a workplace where every individual felt valued, respected, and empowered to thrive.

With a sense of pride and accomplishment, Angela knew that the journey to enhance employee engagement was far from over. But armed with innovative strategies and a commitment to fostering a vibrant workplace culture, BrightWorks Inc. was well on its way to becoming a company where employees could truly thrive and succeed.

Recognition and Rewards

As Angela delved deeper into her quest to enhance employee engagement, she recognized the importance of implementing effective recognition and rewards programs. With a determination to empower and inspire her colleagues, she set out to design innovative approaches to celebrate their contributions and incentivize their performance.

Employee Recognition Programs

Angela convened a meeting with the HR team to discuss the implementation of employee recognition programs at BrightWorks Inc. Together, they brainstormed ideas and developed a framework for acknowledging and celebrating individual and team achievements.

They launched an employee of the month program, where outstanding performers were recognized for their dedication, creativity, and impact on the company. They also implemented peer-to-peer recognition initiatives, allowing colleagues to nominate and applaud each other for their contributions.

But Angela knew that recognition was not just about awards and accolades; it was about creating a culture where every individual felt valued and appreciated. They encouraged managers to give regular feedback and praise to their team members, fostering a sense of pride and belonging within the organization.

Incentive Structures

In addition to recognition programs, Angela recognized the importance of implementing incentive structures to motivate and reward high performance among employees. They designed a variety of incentive programs, including bonuses, commissions, and profit-sharing schemes, to incentivize employees to go above and beyond in their roles.

But Angela also understood that incentives were not one-size-fits-all; they needed to be tailored to the unique needs and preferences of individual employees. They conducted surveys and focus groups to gather insights into what motivated their colleagues and used this information to design personalized incentive structures that resonated with each individual.

As the days passed, Angela witnessed a transformation within BrightWorks Inc. Employees felt more valued, more motivated, and more engaged in their work. With each recognition and reward they received, they felt a sense of pride and accomplishment, fueling their passion and commitment to the company's success.

With a sense of pride and accomplishment, Angela knew that

the journey to enhance employee engagement was far from over. But armed with innovative recognition and rewards programs, BrightWorks Inc. was well on its way to becoming a company where employees felt appreciated, empowered, and inspired to achieve greatness.

Professional Development

As Angela continued her mission to enhance employee engagement at BrightWorks Inc., she recognized the critical importance of investing in the professional development of her colleagues. With a passion for growth and learning, she set out to design comprehensive training and skill enhancement programs that would empower employees to reach their full potential.

Training and Skill Enhancement

Angela gathered the HR team to brainstorm ideas for training and skill enhancement programs that would equip employees with the knowledge and tools they needed to succeed in their roles. Together, they developed a curriculum that encompassed a wide range of topics, from technical skills to leadership development.

They launched regular workshops and seminars led by industry experts, covering topics such as project management, communication skills, and innovation. They also provided access to online courses and resources, allowing employees to learn at their own pace and on their own schedule.

But Angela knew that training was only half the equation; it was essential to provide opportunities for employees to apply their newfound skills in real-world situations. They encouraged employees to take on stretch assignments and cross-functional projects, giving them the opportunity to put their skills into practice and gain valuable experience.

Career Growth Opportunities

In addition to training and skill enhancement programs, Angela recognized the importance of providing clear pathways for career growth and advancement within the company. They developed a career development framework that outlined various career paths and progression opportunities available to employees.

They launched mentorship programs, pairing junior employees with seasoned professionals who could provide guidance and support as they navigated their career paths. They also introduced rotational programs that allowed employees to gain exposure to different departments and roles, broadening their skill sets and perspectives.

But Angela knew that career growth was not just about climbing the corporate ladder; it was about finding fulfillment and purpose in one's work. They conducted career coaching sessions and personality assessments to help employees identify their strengths, interests, and goals, guiding them towards roles that aligned with their aspirations.

As the days passed, Angela witnessed a transformation within BrightWorks Inc. Employees felt more empowered, more motivated, and more invested in their own development. With each training session and career opportunity they pursued, they grew more confident and capable, fueling their passion and commitment to the company's mission.

With a sense of pride and accomplishment, Angela knew that the journey to enhance employee engagement was far from over. But armed with comprehensive professional development programs and clear pathways for career growth, BrightWorks Inc. was well on its way to becoming a company where employees could thrive and succeed.

6

Chapter Six: Strategies for Customer Engagement

As Angela continued her mission to balance employee happiness and customer satisfaction at BrightWorks Inc., she turned her attention to exploring innovative strategies for engaging and delighting customers. With a commitment to building lasting relationships and fostering loyalty, she embarked on a journey to design strategies that would captivate and inspire BrightWorks Inc.'s customer base.

Angela convened a meeting with the marketing and customer service teams, eager to brainstorm ideas and develop a comprehensive plan for enhancing customer engagement. Together, they delved into research, analyzed market trends, and drew upon their own experiences to craft a series of strategies aimed at creating meaningful connections with customers.

1. **Personalized Communication**: Angela understood the importance of treating customers as individuals and tailoring communication to their unique needs and preferences. They developed personalized email campaigns, targeted

CHAPTER SIX: STRATEGIES FOR CUSTOMER ENGAGEMENT

social media ads, and customized product recommendations, creating opportunities to engage with customers on a personal level and build rapport.

2. **Interactive Customer Experiences**: Angela recognized the power of interactive experiences in capturing the attention and imagination of customers. They launched interactive product demos, virtual reality experiences, and gamified challenges, inviting customers to immerse themselves in the world of BrightWorks Inc. and discover the value of its products firsthand.

3. **Proactive Customer Support**: Angela believed that proactive customer support was essential to building trust and loyalty among customers. They implemented proactive outreach programs, monitoring customer feedback and reaching out to customers proactively to address any concerns or issues before they escalated.

4. **Community Building**: Angela understood the importance of fostering a sense of community among BrightWorks Inc.'s customer base. They launched online forums, customer advisory boards, and user groups, providing platforms for customers to connect with each other, share their experiences, and provide valuable feedback to the company.

5. **Surprise and Delight**: Angela knew that sometimes, the little things could make the biggest impact on customer engagement. They implemented surprise and delight initiatives, sending personalized thank-you notes, exclusive discounts, and unexpected gifts to customers as tokens of appreciation for their loyalty and support.

As the days passed, Angela witnessed a transformation within

BrightWorks Inc. Customers felt more connected, more engaged, and more enthusiastic about the company and its products. With each strategy they implemented, they deepened their relationship with customers and strengthened their commitment to delivering exceptional experiences.

With a sense of pride and accomplishment, Angela knew that the journey to enhance customer engagement was far from over. But armed with innovative strategies and a commitment to building lasting relationships, BrightWorks Inc. was well on its way to becoming a company that customers not only loved but also felt truly connected to.

Personalization

As Angela delved deeper into her quest to enhance customer engagement at BrightWorks Inc., she recognized the critical importance of personalization in creating meaningful connections with customers. With a dedication to understanding and meeting the unique needs of each individual, she set out to design strategies that would tailor experiences to customer preferences and foster a deeper sense of connection.

Tailoring Experiences to Customer Preferences

Angela convened a meeting with the marketing and customer experience teams to discuss the implementation of personalized experiences at BrightWorks Inc. Together, they brainstormed ideas and developed a framework for tailoring interactions to customer preferences.

They analyzed customer data to identify patterns and trends, gaining insights into the preferences, behaviors, and interests of their target audience. Armed with this knowledge, they developed personalized marketing campaigns, product recommendations, and communications that resonated with each customer on a personal level.

From customized email newsletters to targeted promotions based on past purchases, Angela and her team sought to create experiences that felt tailor-made for each individual customer. They understood that by speaking directly to their customers' interests and preferences, they could capture their attention and inspire their loyalty.

Data-driven Personalization

But Angela knew that personalization was not just about intuition; it was about leveraging data to inform decision-making and drive results. They implemented data-driven personalization techniques, using advanced analytics and machine learning algorithms to segment customers, predict their needs, and deliver targeted experiences in real-time.

They tracked customer interactions across multiple touchpoints, from website visits to social media engagement to purchase history, capturing valuable data insights at every step of the customer journey. They used this data to personalize product recommendations, content recommendations, and even pricing strategies, ensuring that each customer received a truly personalized experience.

As the days passed, Angela witnessed a transformation within BrightWorks Inc. Customers felt more valued, more understood, and more connected to the company and its products. With each personalized interaction they received, they deepened their relationship with the brand and became more loyal advocates for its products and services.

With a sense of pride and accomplishment, Angela knew that the journey to enhance customer engagement was far from over. But armed with personalized experiences and data-driven insights, BrightWorks Inc. was well on its way to becoming a company that not only met but exceeded the expectations of its customers, one personalized interaction at a time.

Community Building

As Angela delved deeper into her mission to enhance customer engagement at BrightWorks Inc., she understood the power of community building in fostering strong connections and creating loyal brand advocates. With a commitment to nurturing a sense of belonging among customers, she set out to design strategies that would empower them to become ambassadors for the brand and amplify its reach.

Creating Brand Advocates

Angela convened a meeting with the marketing and social media teams to discuss the implementation of community building initiatives at BrightWorks Inc. Together, they brainstormed ideas and developed a plan to turn satisfied customers into passionate brand advocates.

They launched a customer ambassador program, inviting loyal customers to join an exclusive community where they could share their experiences, provide feedback, and participate in special events and promotions. They empowered these brand advocates to spread the word about BrightWorks Inc. through word-of-mouth referrals, social media posts, and online reviews, leveraging their influence to attract new customers and build brand awareness.

But Angela knew that creating brand advocates was not just about incentivizing customers; it was about creating genuine connections and fostering a sense of camaraderie among likeminded individuals. They organized meetups, networking events, and online forums where customers could connect with each other, share their stories, and forge meaningful relationships based on their shared love for BrightWorks Inc. and its products.

Leveraging User-generated Content

In addition to building a community of brand advocates, Angela recognized the power of user-generated content in engaging customers and driving authenticity. They encouraged customers to share their experiences with BrightWorks Inc. through photos, videos, and testimonials, providing them with a platform to showcase their creativity and passion for the brand.

They curated user-generated content on social media channels, website galleries, and marketing materials, amplifying the voices of their customers and showcasing their stories to a wider audience. They also launched hashtag campaigns and contests to encourage participation and incentivize customers to create and share content that reflected their love for BrightWorks Inc.

As the days passed, Angela witnessed a transformation within BrightWorks Inc. Customers felt more connected, more engaged, and more invested in the brand and its community. With each interaction they had and each piece of content they shared, they became more than just customers - they became ambassadors for the brand, spreading the word and championing its mission to the world.

With a sense of pride and accomplishment, Angela knew that the journey to enhance customer engagement was far from over. But armed with a thriving community of brand advocates and a wealth of user-generated content, BrightWorks Inc. was well on its way to becoming a company that not only met but exceeded the expectations of its customers, one passionate advocate at a time.

7

Chapter Seven: Measuring Engagement

As Angela continued her journey to balance employee happiness and customer satisfaction at BrightWorks Inc., she understood the importance of measuring engagement to gauge the effectiveness of their strategies and initiatives. With a commitment to data-driven decision-making, she set out to design a comprehensive approach to measuring engagement that would provide insights into the health of both the employee and customer experience.

Angela convened a meeting with the data analytics team, eager to brainstorm ideas and develop a robust measurement framework for assessing engagement at BrightWorks Inc. Together, they delved into research, analyzed industry best practices, and drew upon their own expertise to craft a series of metrics and key performance indicators (KPIs) that would capture the essence of engagement.

1. **Employee Engagement Metrics**: Angela recognized that engaged employees were the cornerstone of a successful

organization, so they developed a set of metrics to measure employee engagement. This included employee satisfaction surveys, turnover rates, and absenteeism rates, as well as more qualitative measures such as feedback from performance reviews and employee sentiment analysis.

2. **Customer Engagement Metrics**: In addition to measuring employee engagement, Angela understood the importance of assessing customer engagement to understand their level of satisfaction and loyalty. They developed a variety of metrics to measure customer engagement, including Net Promoter Score (NPS), customer satisfaction surveys, retention rates, and customer lifetime value (CLV).

3. **Digital Engagement Metrics**: With an increasing emphasis on digital channels, Angela knew that measuring digital engagement was essential to understanding how customers and employees interacted with BrightWorks Inc. online. They tracked metrics such as website traffic, social media engagement, email open rates, and online reviews to gauge digital engagement and identify areas for improvement.

4. **Qualitative Feedback**: But Angela also recognized that engagement was not just about numbers; it was about understanding the thoughts, feelings, and perceptions of employees and customers. They collected qualitative feedback through focus groups, one-on-one interviews, and open-ended survey questions, providing valuable insights into the drivers of engagement and areas for improvement.

As the days passed, Angela and her team diligently collected and analyzed data to measure engagement at BrightWorks Inc. With each metric they tracked and each insight they uncovered, they gained a deeper understanding of the factors that influenced employee and customer engagement, guiding their decisions and actions as they continued their journey to create a workplace and customer experience that truly resonated with their stakeholders.

With a sense of pride and accomplishment, Angela knew that the journey to measure engagement was far from over. But armed with a comprehensive measurement framework and a commitment to continuous improvement, BrightWorks Inc. was well-equipped to monitor and enhance engagement levels, ensuring that both employees and customers felt valued, satisfied, and engaged in their journey with the company.

Key Performance Indicators (KPIs)

As Angela delved deeper into her mission to measure engagement at BrightWorks Inc., she recognized the importance of identifying key performance indicators (KPIs) that would provide actionable insights into the health of both employee engagement and customer satisfaction. With a commitment to data-driven decision-making, she set out to define KPIs that would serve as barometers of success for the company's engagement initiatives.

Employee Engagement Metrics

Angela understood that engaged employees were the lifeblood of BrightWorks Inc., so she developed a set of KPIs to measure their level of engagement and satisfaction. These included:

1. **Employee Satisfaction Score (ESS)**: A metric derived from regular employee satisfaction surveys, measuring the overall happiness and contentment of employees with their work environment, culture, and opportunities for growth.
2. **Turnover Rate**: The percentage of employees who leave the company within a given period, providing insights into retention and the effectiveness of engagement efforts in retaining talent.
3. **Absenteeism Rate**: The frequency and duration of employee absences from work, indicating their level of engagement and commitment to their roles.
4. **Employee Net Promoter Score (eNPS)**: A measure of employee loyalty and willingness to recommend BrightWorks Inc. as a place to work to others, reflecting their engagement and advocacy for the company.

Customer Satisfaction Metrics

In addition to measuring employee engagement, Angela recognized the importance of assessing customer satisfaction to gauge their level of engagement and loyalty. She defined a set of KPIs to measure customer satisfaction, including:

1. **Net Promoter Score (NPS)**: A widely-used metric that measures the likelihood of customers to recommend BrightWorks Inc. to others, serving as a proxy for customer satisfaction and loyalty.
2. **Customer Satisfaction Score (CSAT)**: A metric derived from customer satisfaction surveys, measuring their overall satisfaction with their interactions with BrightWorks

Inc. and its products or services.
3. **Retention Rate**: The percentage of customers who continue to do business with BrightWorks Inc. over a given period, indicating their loyalty and satisfaction with the company.
4. **Customer Lifetime Value (CLV)**: A measure of the total value that a customer brings to BrightWorks Inc. over the course of their relationship with the company, reflecting their engagement, loyalty, and potential for future revenue generation.

As the days passed, Angela and her team diligently tracked and analyzed these KPIs, gaining valuable insights into the health of both employee engagement and customer satisfaction at BrightWorks Inc. With each metric they monitored and each trend they identified, they were able to make informed decisions and take targeted actions to enhance engagement and drive success for the company.

With a sense of pride and accomplishment, Angela knew that the journey to measure engagement was far from over. But armed with a comprehensive set of KPIs and a commitment to continuous improvement, BrightWorks Inc. was well-equipped to monitor, evaluate, and enhance engagement levels across the organization, ensuring that both employees and customers felt valued, satisfied, and engaged in their journey with the company.

Feedback Mechanisms

As Angela delved deeper into her mission to measure engagement at BrightWorks Inc., she understood the importance of establishing robust feedback mechanisms to gather insights from both employees and customers. With a commitment to fostering open communication and continuous improvement, she set out to design feedback loops that would provide valuable insights into the factors driving engagement and satisfaction.

Surveys and Feedback Loops

Angela convened a meeting with the HR and customer experience teams to discuss the implementation of surveys and feedback loops at BrightWorks Inc. Together, they brainstormed ideas and developed a plan to gather feedback from employees and customers on a regular basis.

For employees, they launched regular engagement surveys, pulse surveys, and exit interviews to gather feedback on various aspects of their experience with BrightWorks Inc. From satisfaction with their role and team dynamics to perceptions of leadership and opportunities for growth, these surveys provided valuable insights into the drivers of engagement and areas for improvement.

For customers, they implemented customer satisfaction surveys, NPS surveys, and feedback forms to gather feedback on their interactions with BrightWorks Inc. From their satisfaction with products and services to their experiences with customer support and brand perception, these surveys provided valuable insights into the factors influencing customer satisfaction and loyalty.

Continuous Improvement Processes

But Angela knew that collecting feedback was only the first step; it was essential to have processes in place to analyze, act upon, and iterate based on the feedback received. They established cross-functional feedback review teams, comprising representatives from various departments, to review survey results and identify key themes and trends.

They developed action plans to address areas for improvement identified through feedback, setting clear goals and timelines for implementation. From enhancing employee training programs to streamlining customer support processes, they took targeted actions to address the root causes of dissatisfaction and drive positive change.

But Angela also recognized that the journey to continuous improvement was ongoing; it required a commitment to iterative learning and adaptation. They monitored the impact of their actions over time, gathering feedback at regular intervals to assess progress and identify new opportunities for improvement.

As the days passed, Angela and her team witnessed the impact of their feedback mechanisms and continuous improvement processes at BrightWorks Inc. With each survey they conducted and each action they took, they saw engagement levels rise, satisfaction scores improve, and relationships with both employees and customers strengthen.

With a sense of pride and accomplishment, Angela knew that the journey to measure engagement was far from over. But armed with robust feedback mechanisms and a commitment to continuous improvement, BrightWorks Inc. was well-equipped to monitor, evaluate, and enhance engagement levels across the organization, ensuring that both employees and customers felt valued, satisfied, and engaged in their journey with the company.

8

Chapter Eight: Building a Culture of Engagement

As Angela continued her journey to balance employee happiness and customer satisfaction at BrightWorks Inc., she understood that creating a culture of engagement was essential to the long-term success of the company. With a dedication to fostering a workplace where employees felt valued, empowered, and inspired, she set out to build a culture of engagement that would permeate every aspect of the organization.

Angela convened a meeting with the leadership team, eager to discuss the importance of building a culture of engagement and the role that each member of the organization played in shaping it. Together, they brainstormed ideas and developed a plan to instill a sense of purpose, belonging, and accountability within the company.

1. **Setting the Tone from the Top**: Angela understood that leadership played a crucial role in shaping the culture of an organization, so she worked closely with senior leaders

to set the tone and lead by example. They communicated openly and transparently with employees, demonstrating their commitment to engagement through their words and actions.

2. **Empowering Employees**: Angela believed that empowered employees were engaged employees, so she encouraged managers to delegate authority and give employees the autonomy to make decisions and take ownership of their work. They fostered a culture of trust and empowerment, where employees felt empowered to innovate, take risks, and drive positive change.

3. **Fostering Collaboration and Teamwork**: Angela recognized the power of collaboration in driving engagement and creativity, so she implemented initiatives to foster collaboration and teamwork across departments. They organized cross-functional projects, team-building activities, and social events, creating opportunities for employees to connect, collaborate, and build relationships.

4. **Celebrating Success and Recognizing Achievements**: Angela understood the importance of celebrating success and recognizing the contributions of employees, so she implemented programs to acknowledge and reward outstanding performance. They celebrated milestones, achievements, and milestones, whether it was through employee of the month awards, peer-to-peer recognition programs, or public acknowledgments during company meetings.

5. **Emphasizing Learning and Development**: Angela believed that learning was essential to engagement and growth, so she invested in the development and upskilling of employees. They provided access to training programs,

mentorship opportunities, and resources for personal and professional development, empowering employees to expand their skills and advance their careers.

As the days passed, Angela and her team worked tirelessly to build a culture of engagement at BrightWorks Inc. With each initiative they implemented and each conversation they had, they saw engagement levels rise, morale improve, and relationships strengthen.

With a sense of pride and accomplishment, Angela knew that the journey to build a culture of engagement was far from over. But armed with a clear vision, strong leadership, and a commitment to fostering a workplace where employees felt valued, empowered, and inspired, BrightWorks Inc. was well on its way to becoming a company where engagement was not just a buzzword but a way of life.

Leadership Commitment

As Angela delved deeper into her mission to build a culture of engagement at BrightWorks Inc., she understood the critical role that leadership commitment played in shaping the organization's culture. With a dedication to leading by example and fostering a culture of trust, she set out to empower leaders at all levels to champion engagement and inspire their teams.

Leading by Example

Angela knew that leadership commitment started at the top, so she worked closely with senior leaders to ensure they embodied the values of engagement and served as role models for the rest of the organization. They led by example, demonstrating their commitment to engagement through their actions, decisions, and behaviors.

They prioritized open communication, transparency, and integrity in all their interactions with employees, fostering an environment where honesty, respect, and collaboration thrived. They were visible and approachable, making themselves available to listen to employee feedback, address concerns, and celebrate successes.

But Angela also recognized that leadership commitment was not just about what leaders said or did; it was about the values they espoused and the culture they fostered within their teams. They encouraged leaders to lead with empathy, compassion, and humility, creating a culture where employees felt valued, respected, and supported in their growth and development.

Fostering a Culture of Trust

In addition to leading by example, Angela emphasized the importance of fostering a culture of trust within the organization. They encouraged leaders to build trust with their teams through consistency, reliability, and accountability, ensuring that promises made were promises kept.

They empowered leaders to delegate authority and give employees the autonomy to make decisions and take ownership of their work. They fostered a culture of psychological safety, where employees felt comfortable speaking up, sharing ideas, and taking risks without fear of retribution or judgment.

As the days passed, Angela and her team witnessed the impact of leadership commitment on the culture of engagement at BrightWorks Inc. With each leader who embraced the values of engagement and demonstrated their commitment to fostering a culture of trust, they saw engagement levels rise, morale improve, and relationships strengthen.

With a sense of pride and accomplishment, Angela knew that the journey to build a culture of engagement was far from over. But armed with strong leadership commitment and a dedication to fostering trust and transparency, BrightWorks Inc. was well on its way to becoming a company where engagement was not just a goal but a fundamental aspect of its identity and success.

Employee Empowerment

As Angela continued her mission to build a culture of engagement at BrightWorks Inc., she recognized the transformative power of empowering employees to drive change and take ownership of their work. With a commitment to fostering a culture of innovation and initiative, she set out to empower employees at all levels to make meaningful contributions and drive positive change within the organization.

Empowering Employees to Drive Change

Angela knew that engaged employees were those who felt empowered to make a difference and contribute to the success of the organization. She encouraged leaders to empower their teams to identify areas for improvement, propose solutions, and take action to drive change.

They implemented suggestion programs, idea incubators, and innovation challenges, providing employees with platforms to share their ideas, collaborate with colleagues, and implement innovative solutions to address business challenges.

Encouraging Innovation and Initiative

In addition to empowering employees to drive change, Angela emphasized the importance of encouraging innovation and initiative within the organization. They fostered a culture of creativity, curiosity, and experimentation, where employees were encouraged to challenge the status quo, think outside the box, and pursue new ideas and opportunities.

They launched innovation labs, hackathons, and brainstorming sessions, providing employees with opportunities to explore new technologies, develop innovative solutions, and prototype new products and services.

But Angela also recognized that fostering innovation and initiative required more than just providing opportunities; it required creating an environment where employees felt supported, encouraged, and inspired to take risks and pursue their passions.

They celebrated and rewarded employees who demonstrated initiative and creativity, whether it was through recognition programs, promotions, or special projects. They encouraged leaders to provide mentorship and support to employees, helping them navigate challenges, overcome obstacles, and bring their ideas to fruition.

As the days passed, Angela and her team witnessed the impact of employee empowerment on the culture of engagement at BrightWorks Inc. With each employee who felt empowered to drive change and pursue innovation, they saw engagement levels rise, morale improve, and the company's ability to adapt and thrive in a rapidly changing world.

With a sense of pride and accomplishment, Angela knew that the journey to build a culture of engagement was far from over. But armed with a commitment to empowering employees and encouraging innovation and initiative, BrightWorks Inc. was well on its way to becoming a company where every individual felt valued, inspired, and empowered to make a difference.

9

Chapter Nine: Aligning Employee and Customer Engagement Strategies

In the heart of BrightWorks Inc., Angela gathered her team to tackle the challenge of aligning employee and customer engagement strategies. She knew that synchronizing these two critical aspects was key to unlocking the company's full potential and delivering exceptional experiences to both employees and customers.

With a determined gleam in her eye, Angela began the discussion, emphasizing the importance of aligning employee and customer engagement strategies to create a seamless and harmonious experience for all.

1. **Understanding the Interconnection**: Angela emphasized that the success of customer engagement relied heavily on the engagement and satisfaction of employees. Happy and motivated employees were more likely to deliver exceptional service and foster positive relationships with customers.
2. **Shared Values and Mission**: Angela highlighted the sig-

nificance of aligning employee and customer engagement strategies with the company's values and mission. When employees and customers shared common values and beliefs, it created a strong sense of community and loyalty, driving engagement and satisfaction.
3. **Communication and Collaboration**: Angela stressed the importance of fostering communication and collaboration between employees and customers. By breaking down silos and encouraging open dialogue, the company could gain valuable insights from both sides, leading to more informed decision-making and better-aligned engagement strategies.
4. **Feedback Loop**: Angela emphasized the need for a feedback loop between employees and customers, where insights from one group informed the actions of the other. By listening to the voices of employees and customers alike, the company could identify areas for improvement and implement targeted strategies to enhance engagement and satisfaction.

As Angela led the team through a spirited discussion, they brainstormed ideas and shared insights, each member contributing their unique perspective and expertise. With a shared sense of purpose and determination, they committed to aligning employee and customer engagement strategies to create a workplace and customer experience that exceeded expectations.

With their minds ablaze with possibilities, Angela and the team set out to integrate these insights into their engagement strategies, confident that by aligning the efforts of employees and customers, they could propel BrightWorks Inc. to new heights of success. As they embarked on this journey of alignment and collaboration, they knew that together, they could achieve anything.

Cross-functional Collaboration

As Angela continued to guide her team through the challenge of aligning employee and customer engagement strategies, she emphasized the importance of cross-functional collaboration in breaking down silos and integrating strategies across the organization.

Breaking Silos

Angela recognized that silos could hinder communication and collaboration between different departments, preventing the alignment of employee and customer engagement strategies. She urged the team to break down these barriers and foster a culture of openness and collaboration, where information flowed freely and ideas were shared across departments.

Angela encouraged the team to organize cross-functional workshops and brainstorming sessions, bringing together employees from different departments to collaborate on engagement initiatives. By breaking down silos and encouraging cross-functional collaboration, the team could leverage diverse perspectives and expertise to develop more comprehensive and integrated strategies.

Integrated Strategies

Angela emphasized the importance of integrating employee and customer engagement strategies to create a seamless and cohesive experience for both groups. She encouraged the team to look for opportunities to align engagement initiatives across the employee and customer journey, ensuring consistency and coherence in messaging and actions.

Angela highlighted examples of companies that had successfully integrated their employee and customer engagement strategies, such as aligning employee training programs with customer service standards or involving frontline employees in the design of customer experiences. These companies recognized that by integrating their efforts, they could create a more holistic and impactful engagement experience for both employees and customers.

As Angela concluded her discussion on cross-functional collaboration and integrated strategies, the team nodded in agreement, recognizing the importance of working together to achieve alignment and synergy across the organization. With a renewed commitment to collaboration and integration, they set out to break down silos and align their employee and customer engagement strategies, confident that by working together, they could create a workplace and customer experience that truly set BrightWorks Inc. apart.

Co-creation

As Angela delved deeper into the discussion of aligning employee and customer engagement strategies, she introduced the concept of co-creation—a powerful approach to collaborative innovation that involved engaging customers in the product development process.

Collaborative Innovation

Angela emphasized the importance of involving customers in the innovation process, recognizing that they held valuable insights and perspectives that could drive the development of products and services that truly met their needs and preferences. She urged the team to embrace a mindset of openness and curiosity, welcoming feedback and ideas from customers at every stage of the product lifecycle.

Angela shared examples of companies that had successfully embraced co-creation, involving customers in everything from ideation and design to testing and refinement. These companies recognized that by collaborating with customers, they could create products and services that were more innovative, relevant, and impactful.

Engaging Customers in Product Development

Angela outlined strategies for engaging customers in the product development process, including:

1. **Customer Feedback Platforms**: Angela encouraged the team to establish channels for collecting feedback from customers, such as surveys, focus groups, and online forums. By listening to the voice of the customer, the team could gain valuable insights into their preferences, pain points, and unmet needs.
2. **Co-design Workshops**: Angela suggested organizing

co-design workshops where customers could collaborate with employees to generate ideas and concepts for new products and services. By involving customers in the design process, the team could ensure that products were tailored to their specific needs and preferences.

3. **Beta Testing Programs**: Angela recommended implementing beta testing programs where customers could try out new products and provide feedback on their usability, functionality, and performance. By involving customers in the testing phase, the team could identify any issues or opportunities for improvement before products were launched to the wider market.

As Angela concluded her discussion on co-creation, the team felt energized and inspired by the possibilities of engaging customers in the product development process. With a renewed commitment to collaboration and innovation, they set out to embrace co-creation as a core component of their strategy for aligning employee and customer engagement strategies, confident that by working together with customers, they could drive meaningful change and create products and services that truly delighted and empowered them.

10

Chapter Ten: Overcoming Challenges

As Angela and the team at BrightWorks Inc. continued their journey to build a culture of engagement, they encountered various challenges along the way. From unexpected setbacks to resistance to change, they faced obstacles that tested their resolve and determination. But with a shared commitment to their mission and a spirit of resilience, they embraced these challenges as opportunities for growth and learning.

One of the challenges they faced was resistance to change from some employees who were comfortable with the status quo. Despite their best efforts to communicate the benefits of engagement initiatives, some employees were hesitant to embrace change and adapt to new ways of working.

Angela and her team responded to this challenge by doubling down on their communication efforts, engaging in open and transparent dialogue with employees to address their concerns and fears. They emphasized the importance of change as a catalyst for growth and innovation, highlighting the positive impact it would have on both the company and its employees.

Another challenge they encountered was the need to balance short-term goals with long-term vision. In the fast-paced business environment, it was tempting to prioritize immediate results over long-term sustainability. But Angela knew that building a culture of engagement required patience and persistence, and that meaningful change took time.

They developed strategies to strike a balance between short-term wins and long-term goals, setting achievable milestones and celebrating progress along the way. They reminded employees of the company's vision and values, reinforcing their commitment to building a workplace where employees felt valued, empowered, and inspired.

But perhaps the greatest challenge they faced was the external pressures and uncertainties of the business world. From economic downturns to industry disruptions, they navigated through turbulent times that threatened to derail their progress and undermine their efforts.

Angela and her team responded to these challenges with agility and adaptability, embracing change as an opportunity to innovate and reinvent themselves. They remained focused on their core values and mission, using them as guiding principles to navigate through uncertainty and adversity.

As the days passed, Angela and her team learned valuable lessons from overcoming challenges at BrightWorks Inc. Each obstacle they faced strengthened their resolve, deepened their commitment, and brought them closer together as a team.

With a sense of pride and accomplishment, Angela knew that the journey to build a culture of engagement was far from over. But armed with resilience, determination, and a shared sense of purpose, BrightWorks Inc. was well-equipped to overcome any challenges that lay ahead and continue their journey towards building a workplace where engagement thrived, and success flourished.

Resistance to Change

As Angela and the team at BrightWorks Inc. confronted the challenge of resistance to change, they recognized the importance of addressing this obstacle head-on. Despite their efforts to cultivate a culture of engagement, they encountered pockets of resistance from employees who were hesitant to embrace new initiatives and ways of working.

Addressing Resistance

Angela and her team understood that resistance to change often stemmed from fear of the unknown, uncertainty about the future, and discomfort with leaving behind familiar routines. They approached this challenge with empathy and understanding, recognizing that change could be unsettling for many individuals.

They engaged in open and honest conversations with employees to understand their concerns and address any misconceptions or fears they may have had. They emphasized the importance of transparency and communication, providing context and clarity around the reasons for change and the benefits it would bring to both individuals and the organization as a whole.

CHAPTER TEN: OVERCOMING CHALLENGES

Change Management Strategies

In addition to addressing resistance through communication and dialogue, Angela and her team implemented change management strategies to support employees through the transition. They provided training and support to help employees develop the skills and capabilities needed to adapt to new ways of working.

They also created opportunities for employees to participate in the change process, involving them in decision-making and soliciting their input and feedback on proposed initiatives. This not only empowered employees to take ownership of the change but also increased their sense of buy-in and commitment to its success.

Furthermore, they recognized the importance of celebrating small victories and milestones along the way, acknowledging the progress made and the efforts of employees who embraced change despite their initial reservations. This helped to build momentum and maintain morale, inspiring others to overcome their resistance and embrace the journey of transformation.

As the days passed, Angela and her team witnessed a gradual shift in mindset as employees began to see the benefits of change and embrace new ways of working. With each conversation they had and each initiative they implemented, they saw resistance give way to acceptance, and skepticism give way to enthusiasm.

With a sense of pride and accomplishment, Angela knew that the journey to overcome resistance to change was far from over. But armed with empathy, communication, and change management strategies, BrightWorks Inc. was well-equipped to navigate through the challenges of transformation and emerge stronger and more resilient on the other side.

Sustaining Engagement

As Angela and the team at BrightWorks Inc. continued their journey to build a culture of engagement, they recognized the importance of sustaining engagement over the long term. They understood that engagement was not a one-time effort but an ongoing commitment that required continuous nurturing and renewal.

Preventing Burnout

One of the challenges they faced in sustaining engagement was preventing burnout among employees. As they poured their energy into driving change and embracing new initiatives, there was a risk of employees becoming overwhelmed and exhausted.

Angela and her team implemented strategies to prevent burnout and promote employee well-being. They encouraged employees to prioritize self-care, setting boundaries around work hours and taking regular breaks to recharge. They provided resources and support for stress management and resilience building, offering workshops, counseling services, and mindfulness programs to help employees cope with the pressures of work.

Furthermore, they promoted a culture of work-life balance, encouraging employees to pursue their passions and interests outside of work. They organized team outings, wellness retreats, and volunteer opportunities, providing opportunities for employees to unwind, recharge, and reconnect with their purpose and passion.

CHAPTER TEN: OVERCOMING CHALLENGES

Renewing Engagement Efforts

In addition to preventing burnout, Angela and her team recognized the importance of renewing engagement efforts to keep momentum going and inspire continued commitment from employees. They understood that engagement was not a one-time achievement but an ongoing journey that required continuous effort and attention.

They launched initiatives to renew engagement efforts, including employee appreciation events, recognition programs, and team-building activities. They celebrated milestones and achievements, acknowledging the contributions of employees who had gone above and beyond in their commitment to the company's mission and values.

They also solicited feedback from employees on a regular basis, asking for their input and ideas on how to further enhance engagement within the organization. They listened to their concerns and suggestions, incorporating their feedback into future initiatives and demonstrating their commitment to creating a workplace where every voice was heard and valued.

As the days passed, Angela and her team witnessed the impact of their efforts to sustain engagement at BrightWorks Inc. With each initiative they launched and each conversation they had, they saw engagement levels rise, morale improves, and relationships strengthen.

With a sense of pride and accomplishment, Angela knew that the journey to sustain engagement was far from over. But armed with strategies to prevent burnout and renew engagement efforts, BrightWorks Inc. was well-equipped to continue its journey towards building a workplace where employees felt valued, empowered, and inspired to make a difference.

11

Chapter Eleven: Case Studies: Best Practices

As Angela and the team at BrightWorks Inc. continued their quest to build a culture of engagement, they sought inspiration and guidance from real-world examples of companies that had successfully implemented engagement initiatives. They understood the value of learning from the experiences of others and sought to identify best practices that could be adapted and applied within their own organization.

Case Study 1: Company X - Building a Culture of Recognition

In the first case study, Angela explored the journey of Company X, a leading technology firm known for its exceptional employee engagement. Company X had implemented a culture of recognition, where employees were regularly acknowledged and rewarded for their contributions.

Angela learned that Company X had established a peer-to-peer recognition program, where employees could nominate their colleagues for recognition based on their contributions to the company's success. They also implemented an employee of the month award, where outstanding performers were recognized and celebrated at company-wide meetings.

By prioritizing recognition and appreciation, Company X had created a culture where employees felt valued, appreciated, and motivated to perform at their best. Angela took notes on the key strategies and tactics employed by Company X and considered how they could be adapted and implemented within BrightWorks Inc.

Case Study 2: Company Y - Fostering a Culture of Innovation

In the second case study, Angela examined the journey of Company Y, a global retailer known for its culture of innovation. Company Y had implemented initiatives to foster creativity, experimentation, and collaboration among its employees.

Angela learned that Company Y had established innovation labs, where employees were encouraged to explore new ideas, prototype new products, and experiment with new technologies. They also organized hackathons and brainstorming sessions, providing employees with opportunities to collaborate across departments and develop innovative solutions to business challenges.

By fostering a culture of innovation, Company Y had created an environment where employees felt empowered to think outside the box, challenge the status quo, and pursue new ideas and opportunities. Angela took note of the strategies and tactics employed by Company Y and considered how they could be adapted and implemented within BrightWorks Inc.

As Angela delved deeper into the case studies, she gained valuable insights and inspiration from the experiences of Company X and Company Y. She recognized that building a culture of engagement was not a one-size-fits-all endeavor but required a tailored approach that aligned with the unique needs and values of BrightWorks Inc.

With a renewed sense of purpose and determination, Angela and her team set out to implement the best practices gleaned from the case studies, confident that they were on the right path towards building a workplace where engagement thrived, and success flourished.

Employee Engagement Success Stories

As Angela delved deeper into her exploration of best practices in employee engagement, she uncovered a treasure trove of success stories from companies renowned for their high employee satisfaction levels. These real-life examples served as beacons of inspiration, illuminating the path forward for BrightWorks Inc. in its quest to build a culture of engagement.

Success Story 1: Google - Cultivating a Culture of Innovation and Collaboration

In the first success story, Angela examined the journey of Google, a global technology giant known for its vibrant and innovative workplace culture. Google had implemented a range of initiatives to foster engagement, including flexible work arrangements, a strong emphasis on employee well-being, and a culture of collaboration and open communication.

Angela learned that Google placed a high value on employee autonomy and empowerment, providing employees with the freedom to pursue their passions and interests. They also fostered a culture of psychological safety, where employees felt comfortable taking risks, sharing ideas, and challenging the status quo without fear of judgment or reprisal.

Lessons Learned:

From Google's success story, Angela gleaned several valuable lessons that could be applied within BrightWorks Inc.:

1. Foster a Culture of Innovation: Encourage creativity, experimentation, and collaboration among employees by providing them with opportunities to explore new ideas, prototype new products, and collaborate across departments.
2. Prioritize Employee Well-being: Recognize the importance of employee well-being and create a supportive work environment that promotes work-life balance, mental health, and physical wellness.
3. Cultivate Psychological Safety: Create a culture where employees feel safe to express their opinions, share ideas, and take risks, fostering a sense of trust, openness, and collaboration within the organization.

Success Story 2: Salesforce - Putting Employees First

In the second success story, Angela explored the journey of Salesforce, a leading customer relationship management company known for its employee-centric culture. Salesforce had implemented a range of initiatives to prioritize employee well-being and satisfaction, including generous benefits packages, opportunities for career development and advancement, and a strong sense of corporate social responsibility.

Angela learned that Salesforce placed a strong emphasis on putting employees first, recognizing that engaged and satisfied employees were essential to the company's success. They invested in programs to support employee growth and development, including mentorship programs, leadership training, and tuition reimbursement.

Lessons Learned:

From Salesforce's success story, Angela identified several key lessons that could be applied within BrightWorks Inc.:

1. Put Employees First: Prioritize the needs and well-being of employees, recognizing that engaged and satisfied employees are essential to the company's success.
2. Invest in Employee Development: Provide opportunities for career development and advancement, including mentorship programs, training opportunities, and tuition reimbursement.
3. Demonstrate Corporate Social Responsibility: Engage employees in meaningful initiatives that align with the company's values and mission, fostering a sense of purpose and pride in their work.

As Angela reflected on the success stories of Google and Salesforce, she felt inspired and energized by the possibilities that lay ahead for BrightWorks Inc. Armed with valuable lessons learned and a renewed sense of purpose, she and her team set out to implement the best practices gleaned from these real-life examples, confident that they were on the right path towards building a workplace where engagement thrived and success flourished.

Customer Engagement Success Stories

As Angela delved further into her exploration of best practices, she turned her attention to success stories in customer engagement. These stories showcased real companies that had built loyal customer bases through innovative strategies and unwavering commitment to customer satisfaction.

Success Story 1: Apple - Creating a Cult-Like Following through Innovation and Brand Loyalty

In the first success story, Angela examined the journey of Apple, a global technology company renowned for its cult-like following and unwavering brand loyalty. Apple had successfully engaged customers through innovative products, seamless user experiences, and a strong emphasis on brand identity and storytelling.

Angela learned that Apple prioritized customer satisfaction and loyalty above all else, investing heavily in research and development to create products that exceeded customer expectations. They also cultivated a strong brand identity and community, fostering a sense of belonging and exclusivity among their customer base.

CHAPTER ELEVEN: CASE STUDIES: BEST PRACTICES

Innovative Customer Engagement Strategies:

From Apple's success story, Angela gleaned several innovative customer engagement strategies that could be applied within BrightWorks Inc.:

1. Focus on Product Innovation: Invest in research and development to create innovative products and services that delight customers and differentiate the brand from competitors.
2. Cultivate Brand Loyalty: Create a strong brand identity and community that resonates with customers, fostering a sense of belonging and exclusivity that encourages repeat purchases and referrals.
3. Embrace Storytelling: Use storytelling to connect with customers on an emotional level, building a narrative around the brand that captures their imagination and inspires loyalty.

Success Story 2: Amazon - Personalizing the Customer Experience through Data-Driven Insights

In the second success story, Angela explored the journey of Amazon, a global e-commerce giant known for its personalized customer experience and relentless focus on customer satisfaction. Amazon had successfully engaged customers through data-driven insights, personalized recommendations, and seamless shopping experiences.

Angela learned that Amazon leveraged advanced analytics and machine learning algorithms to analyze customer data and deliver personalized recommendations and experiences. They also prioritized customer convenience and satisfaction, offering fast shipping, easy returns, and responsive customer support.

Innovative Customer Engagement Strategies:

From Amazon's success story, Angela identified several innovative customer engagement strategies that could be applied within BrightWorks Inc.:

1. Harness the Power of Data: Leverage customer data and insights to personalize the customer experience, delivering targeted recommendations and communications that resonate with individual preferences and behaviors.
2. Prioritize Customer Convenience: Streamline the customer journey and remove friction points, making it easy and convenient for customers to interact with the brand and make purchases.
3. Provide Responsive Customer Support: Offer fast, reliable customer support across multiple channels, ensuring that customers receive assistance whenever they need it and have their concerns addressed promptly and effectively.

As Angela absorbed the success stories of Apple and Amazon, she felt inspired by the innovative strategies and unwavering commitment to customer satisfaction demonstrated by these companies. Armed with valuable insights and ideas, she and her team set out to implement the best practices gleaned from these real-life examples, confident that they were on the right path towards building a company where both employee and customer engagement thrived.

12

Chapter Twelve: Future Trends in Engagement

As Angela and the team at BrightWorks Inc. continued their journey to build a culture of engagement, they cast their gaze towards the future, eager to anticipate emerging trends and adapt to the changing landscape of engagement. In this chapter, Angela explored the exciting possibilities and potential challenges that lay ahead, envisioning a future where engagement thrived and innovation flourished.

Angela gathered the team in the conference room, her eyes sparkling with excitement as she prepared to delve into the future of engagement. She shared her vision for a workplace where employees felt valued, empowered, and inspired to make a difference, and where customers felt deeply connected to the brand and its mission.

1. **Remote Work Revolution**: Angela predicted that remote work would continue to be a dominant trend in the future, driven by advances in technology and shifting attitudes towards work-life balance. She envisioned a

workplace where employees had the flexibility to work from anywhere, leveraging digital tools and platforms to collaborate seamlessly and stay connected with colleagues and customers.

2. **Virtual Reality and Augmented Reality**: Angela imagined a future where virtual reality and augmented reality would revolutionize the way employees engaged with each other and with customers. She envisioned immersive virtual environments where teams could collaborate on projects, conduct virtual meetings, and interact with customers in new and exciting ways.

3. **AI-Powered Personalization**: Angela anticipated that artificial intelligence would play an increasingly important role in personalizing the employee and customer experience. She envisioned AI-powered algorithms that analyzed data to deliver personalized recommendations, communications, and support, tailored to the unique preferences and behaviors of individuals.

4. **Focus on Well-being and Mental Health**: Angela emphasized the growing importance of prioritizing employee well-being and mental health in the future workplace. She envisioned companies implementing programs and initiatives to support employee wellness, including mental health resources, stress management workshops, and mindfulness programs.

5. **Sustainability and Corporate Social Responsibility**: Angela highlighted the rising demand for companies to demonstrate their commitment to sustainability and corporate social responsibility. She envisioned companies integrating environmental and social impact initiatives into their engagement strategies, aligning with the values

and expectations of employees and customers alike.

As Angela painted a vivid picture of the future of engagement, the team listened intently, their imaginations ignited with possibilities. They felt inspired by Angela's vision and energized by the opportunities that lay ahead. With a renewed sense of purpose and determination, they set out to embrace the future of engagement, confident that BrightWorks Inc. was well-equipped to adapt, innovate, and thrive in the ever-evolving landscape of engagement.

Technological Advancements

As Angela delved deeper into the future of engagement, she turned her attention to the transformative impact of technological advancements on the employee and customer experience. She envisioned a future where AI and automation would revolutionize engagement strategies, and virtual and augmented reality would create immersive experiences that transcended physical limitations.

AI and Automation in Engagement

Angela predicted that AI and automation would play a central role in shaping the future of engagement, offering unprecedented opportunities to personalize interactions, streamline processes, and enhance efficiency. She envisioned AI-powered chatbots and virtual assistants that could provide instant support and guidance to employees and customers, freeing up human resources to focus on more complex tasks and strategic initiatives.

She imagined AI algorithms analyzing vast amounts of data to predict employee and customer behavior, enabling companies to anticipate needs, tailor offerings, and deliver personalized experiences at scale. From predictive analytics to machine learning algorithms, Angela saw AI as a powerful tool for unlocking new levels of engagement and satisfaction.

Virtual and Augmented Reality Experiences

Angela's imagination soared as she envisioned a future where virtual and augmented reality would transform the way employees and customers engaged with each other and with the brand. She pictured virtual reality simulations that could immerse employees in realistic training scenarios, allowing them to develop new skills and experiences in a safe and controlled environment.

She also imagined augmented reality experiences that could enhance the customer journey, allowing customers to visualize products in their own space before making a purchase or providing interactive guidance and support in real-time. From virtual showroom experiences to augmented reality product demonstrations, Angela saw endless possibilities for creating memorable and impactful interactions.

As Angela shared her vision of the future with the team, their excitement grew palpable. They marveled at the potential of AI and automation to revolutionize engagement strategies and create personalized experiences that resonated with employees and customers alike. They were equally captivated by the possibilities of virtual and augmented reality to transport them to new worlds and elevate their interactions to new heights.

With a sense of awe and anticipation, Angela and the team

embraced the future of engagement, eager to harness the power of technology to create a workplace and customer experience that surpassed all expectations. As they embarked on this journey into the unknown, they knew that the possibilities were limitless, and the future was theirs to shape.

Evolving Workforce Dynamics

As Angela continued to explore the future of engagement, she turned her attention to the evolving dynamics of the workforce, recognizing the profound impact that remote work trends and the gig economy would have on engagement strategies in the years to come.

Remote Work Trends

Angela foresaw a future where remote work would become the norm rather than the exception, driven by advancements in technology and shifting attitudes towards work-life balance. She envisioned a workforce that was no longer bound by physical office spaces, but instead, empowered to work from anywhere in the world.

She imagined teams collaborating seamlessly across time zones and continents, leveraging digital tools and platforms to communicate, collaborate, and innovate in ways that were previously unimaginable. From virtual team meetings to remote brainstorming sessions, Angela saw remote work as an opportunity to unlock new levels of flexibility, productivity, and engagement.

Gig Economy Implications

Angela also considered the implications of the gig economy on engagement strategies, recognizing the growing trend towards independent work and flexible employment arrangements. She envisioned a future where companies embraced the gig economy as a source of talent and innovation, tapping into a diverse pool of freelancers, contractors, and consultants to supplement their workforce.

She imagined a workforce that was increasingly fluid and dynamic, with individuals moving seamlessly between projects and roles based on their skills, interests, and availability. From project-based assignments to short-term contracts, Angela saw the gig economy as a catalyst for creativity, agility, and adaptability in the future workplace.

As Angela shared her insights with the team, they nodded in agreement, recognizing the profound implications of remote work trends and the gig economy on engagement strategies. They understood that the future of engagement would require a shift in mindset and approach, as they adapted to the changing dynamics of the workforce and embraced new ways of working.

With a sense of anticipation and excitement, Angela and the team embraced the future of engagement, confident that they were prepared to navigate the challenges and opportunities that lay ahead. As they embarked on this journey into the unknown, they knew that they were not alone, but part of a global community of innovators and pioneers shaping the future of work and engagement.

13

Chapter Thirteen: Ethical Considerations

As Angela and the team at BrightWorks Inc. continued to explore the future of engagement, they recognized the importance of ethical considerations in shaping their approach to engagement strategies. In this chapter, Angela delved into the complex and nuanced ethical dilemmas that arose in the pursuit of engagement, grappling with questions of fairness, transparency, and responsibility.

Angela gathered the team in the conference room, her expression serious as she prepared to address the topic of ethical considerations. She emphasized the importance of conducting engagement initiatives with integrity and empathy, ensuring that they aligned with the company's values and respected the rights and dignity of employees and customers alike.

1. **Fairness and Equity**: Angela stressed the importance of fairness and equity in engagement initiatives, recognizing the need to ensure that all employees had equal access to opportunities and resources. She emphasized the

importance of addressing systemic inequalities and biases that may exist within the organization, striving to create a workplace where everyone felt valued, respected, and empowered to succeed.

2. **Transparency and Accountability**: Angela highlighted the importance of transparency and accountability in engagement strategies, emphasizing the need for clear communication and open dialogue with employees and customers. She urged the team to be honest and forthright in their interactions, ensuring that they were transparent about the goals, methods, and outcomes of engagement initiatives.

3. **Privacy and Data Protection**: Angela addressed the ethical considerations surrounding privacy and data protection, recognizing the importance of safeguarding sensitive information and respecting the privacy rights of employees and customers. She emphasized the need to comply with relevant laws and regulations governing data privacy and security, ensuring that data was collected, stored, and used responsibly and ethically.

4. **Social Responsibility**: Angela underscored the company's social responsibility in engagement initiatives, urging the team to consider the broader impact of their actions on society and the environment. She encouraged them to integrate principles of sustainability and corporate social responsibility into their engagement strategies, aligning with the company's values and contributing to positive social change.

As Angela led the team through a thought-provoking discussion on ethical considerations, they nodded in agreement, recognizing the importance of conducting engagement initiatives with integrity and ethics. They understood that while engagement was essential for business success, it must be pursued in a responsible and ethical manner, ensuring that the interests and well-being of employees and customers were always paramount.

With a renewed commitment to ethical engagement, Angela and the team set out to integrate these considerations into their engagement strategies, confident that they were on the right path towards building a workplace and customer experience that was not only engaging but also ethical and responsible. As they embarked on this journey, they knew that they were not only shaping the future of engagement but also setting a positive example for others to follow.

Privacy and Data Security

As Angela delved deeper into the ethical considerations surrounding engagement strategies, she turned her attention to the critical issue of privacy and data security. Recognizing the importance of safeguarding sensitive information, Angela emphasized the need to protect both customer data and employee privacy rights.

Protecting Customer Data

Angela stressed the importance of protecting customer data as a fundamental ethical responsibility. She highlighted the trust that customers placed in the company to handle their information with care and respect, and the potential consequences of a data breach or misuse.

Angela outlined the company's commitment to compliance with relevant laws and regulations governing data privacy and security, such as GDPR and CCPA. She emphasized the importance of implementing robust security measures, such as encryption, access controls, and regular security audits, to protect customer data from unauthorized access or disclosure.

Angela also emphasized the importance of transparency and accountability in the company's data handling practices, ensuring that customers were informed about how their data was being used and giving them control over their privacy preferences. She urged the team to prioritize the protection of customer data in all engagement initiatives, demonstrating the company's commitment to ethical conduct and trustworthiness.

Employee Privacy Rights

In addition to protecting customer data, Angela also addressed the importance of respecting employee privacy rights. She recognized that employees had a right to privacy in the workplace, and that their personal information should be handled with the same care and respect as customer data.

Angela emphasized the need to establish clear policies and procedures for handling employee data, ensuring that it was collected, stored, and used in compliance with applicable laws and regulations. She highlighted the importance of obtaining informed consent from employees before collecting any personal information and giving them control over how their data was used.

Angela also stressed the importance of transparency and communication with employees about their privacy rights and the company's data handling practices. She encouraged the team to foster a culture of trust and openness, where employees felt comfortable raising concerns about privacy and data security and confident that their rights would be respected.

As Angela concluded her discussion on privacy and data security, the team nodded in agreement, recognizing the critical importance of protecting both customer data and employee privacy rights. With a renewed commitment to ethical conduct and responsible engagement, they set out to implement robust policies and procedures to safeguard sensitive information and build trust with both customers and employees alike.

Fairness and Equity

As Angela continued her exploration of ethical considerations, she turned her attention to the critical issue of fairness and equity in engagement practices. Recognizing the importance of addressing bias and ensuring equal opportunities for all, Angela emphasized the company's commitment to creating a workplace where every employee felt valued, respected, and empowered to succeed.

Addressing Bias in Engagement Practices

Angela acknowledged the existence of unconscious bias in engagement practices and the potential impact it could have on decision-making processes. She urged the team to be vigilant in identifying and addressing bias in all aspects of engagement, from recruitment and performance evaluations to rewards and recognition.

Angela outlined strategies for mitigating bias, including implementing objective criteria and standardized processes, providing diversity and unconscious bias training for employees, and fostering a culture of inclusivity and belonging where diverse perspectives were valued and respected.

Ensuring Equal Opportunities for All

In addition to addressing bias, Angela emphasized the importance of ensuring equal opportunities for all employees. She recognized that systemic inequalities and barriers to advancement could prevent certain groups from fully participating and thriving in the workplace.

Angela outlined the company's commitment to diversity, equity, and inclusion, emphasizing the importance of creating a level playing field where everyone had the opportunity to succeed based on their skills, abilities, and contributions. She encouraged the team to prioritize diversity and inclusion in all aspects of engagement, from recruitment and promotion to training and development.

Angela also stressed the importance of fostering a supportive and inclusive work environment where employees felt valued, respected, and empowered to bring their whole selves to work. She encouraged the team to listen to the voices of underrepresented groups and take action to address their needs and concerns, ensuring that the company was truly inclusive and equitable for all.

As Angela concluded her discussion on fairness and equity, the team nodded in agreement, recognizing the importance of creating a workplace where every employee had an equal opportunity to succeed. With a renewed commitment to diversity, equity, and inclusion, they set out to implement policies and practices that would ensure fairness and equity in all aspects of engagement, building a workplace where everyone could thrive and succeed.

14

Chapter Fourteen: Global Perspectives on Engagement

As Angela and the team at BrightWorks Inc. continued their exploration of engagement, they recognized the importance of considering global perspectives to ensure that their strategies were relevant and effective in diverse cultural contexts. In this chapter, Angela delved into the unique challenges and opportunities of engagement on a global scale, drawing inspiration from different cultures and regions around the world.

Angela gathered the team in the conference room, her eyes alight with curiosity as she prepared to discuss global perspectives on engagement. She emphasized the importance of embracing diversity and cultural sensitivity in engagement strategies, recognizing that what worked in one region may not necessarily work in another.

1. **Cultural Diversity**: Angela highlighted the richness of cultural diversity around the world and the importance of understanding and respecting cultural differences in

engagement practices. She encouraged the team to be open-minded and adaptable, recognizing that engagement strategies that were effective in one culture may need to be modified or adapted to fit the cultural norms and values of another.
2. **Regional Differences**: Angela explored the unique challenges and opportunities of engagement in different regions around the world. From the collectivist cultures of Asia to the individualistic cultures of North America, Angela emphasized the importance of tailoring engagement strategies to fit the specific needs and preferences of each region.
3. **Language and Communication**: Angela addressed the importance of language and communication in engagement efforts, recognizing that effective communication was essential for building trust and rapport with employees and customers alike. She encouraged the team to consider language preferences and cultural nuances in their communication strategies, ensuring that messages resonated with their intended audience.
4. **Global Citizenship**: Angela underscored the importance of being good global citizens in engagement efforts, recognizing that companies had a responsibility to contribute positively to the communities in which they operated. She encouraged the team to consider the social, environmental, and ethical implications of their engagement initiatives, striving to make a positive impact on a global scale.

As Angela led the team through a thought-provoking discussion on global perspectives on engagement, they listened intently, eager to learn from different cultures and regions around the world. They recognized the importance of embracing diversity and cultural sensitivity in their engagement efforts, striving to create a workplace and customer experience that resonated with people from all walks of life.

With a renewed commitment to global engagement, Angela and the team set out to integrate these perspectives into their strategies, confident that they were on the right path towards building a company that was not only successful but also culturally aware and inclusive. As they embarked on this journey, they knew that they were not only shaping the future of engagement but also contributing to a more connected and understanding world.

Cultural Differences

As Angela delved deeper into the topic of global engagement, she focused on the profound influence of cultural differences on engagement practices. She recognized that understanding and respecting these cultural nuances was essential for building effective engagement strategies that resonated with people from diverse backgrounds.

Cultural Influences on Engagement

Angela emphasized the importance of recognizing the cultural influences that shape attitudes towards work, communication styles, and expectations for engagement. She highlighted examples of how cultural values such as collectivism versus individualism, hierarchy versus egalitarianism, and direct versus indirect communication could impact engagement practices in different regions.

Angela encouraged the team to conduct thorough research and engage in cross-cultural training to deepen their understanding of cultural differences and adapt their engagement strategies accordingly. She stressed the importance of being sensitive to cultural nuances and avoiding assumptions or stereotypes that could lead to misunderstandings or miscommunication.

Globalization Challenges

In addition to cultural differences, Angela also addressed the challenges posed by globalization in the context of engagement. She recognized that as companies expanded their operations into new markets and regions, they encountered increasingly diverse and complex cultural landscapes.

Angela emphasized the importance of agility and flexibility in responding to the challenges of globalization, recognizing that engagement strategies that were effective in one market may not necessarily translate to success in another. She encouraged the team to be proactive in seeking feedback from local stakeholders, adapting their strategies based on local preferences and cultural norms.

Angela also highlighted the need for companies to demonstrate cultural competence and humility in their engagement efforts, acknowledging that they were guests in the communities where they operated and striving to build trust and rapport through respectful and authentic interactions.

As Angela concluded her discussion on cultural differences and globalization challenges, the team nodded in agreement, recognizing the importance of embracing diversity and cultural sensitivity in their engagement strategies. With a renewed commitment to cross-cultural understanding and adaptation, they set out to build engagement practices that honored and celebrated the rich tapestry of cultures and perspectives around the world.

Regional Trends

As Angela continued her exploration of global engagement, she shifted her focus to regional trends, examining the unique engagement strategies that had emerged in different parts of the world. She recognized that while there were universal principles of engagement, there were also regional nuances and preferences that influenced how engagement was practiced.

Engagement Strategies in Different Regions

Angela delved into the various engagement strategies that had proven successful in different regions around the world. From the collaborative and relationship-driven approach of Asian cultures to the performance-driven and merit-based approach of Western cultures, Angela highlighted the diversity of approaches to engagement.

In Asia, Angela noted the importance of building strong relationships and trust with employees and customers, often through social gatherings, team-building activities, and personalized interactions. In contrast, in North America, she observed a focus on individual achievement and recognition, with performance-based incentives and rewards driving engagement.

Angela also explored the emerging trends in engagement in regions such as Latin America, Africa, and the Middle

East, recognizing the influence of cultural, economic, and social factors on engagement practices. She encouraged the team to learn from these diverse perspectives and adapt their engagement strategies accordingly, recognizing that what worked in one region may not necessarily work in another.

Lessons from Global Markets

Drawing on insights from global markets, Angela highlighted key lessons that could be applied to engagement practices worldwide. She emphasized the importance of flexibility and agility in responding to local preferences and cultural norms, recognizing that successful engagement required a nuanced and context-specific approach.

Angela urged the team to adopt a mindset of continuous learning and adaptation, seeking inspiration from global markets and integrating best practices into their own engagement strategies. She encouraged them to embrace diversity and inclusivity, recognizing that a one-size-fits-all approach to engagement was unlikely to be effective in today's globalized world.

As Angela concluded her discussion on regional trends and lessons from global markets, the team nodded in agreement, recognizing the value of learning from diverse perspectives and experiences. With a newfound appreciation for the richness of global engagement, they set out to integrate these insights into their own engagement practices, confident that they were on the right path towards building a workplace and customer experience that resonated with people from all corners of the globe.

15

Chapter Fifteen: The Engagement Equation in Action

As Angela and the team at BrightWorks Inc. neared the end of their journey to understand and implement effective engagement strategies, they were eager to put their knowledge into action. In this final chapter, Angela showcased real-world examples of how the engagement equation had been applied successfully, demonstrating its transformative power in driving employee happiness and customer satisfaction.

Angela gathered the team in the conference room one last time, her heart filled with pride as she prepared to share the stories of success that had emerged from their journey. She emphasized the importance of perseverance, creativity, and collaboration in bringing the engagement equation to life, and she urged the team to take inspiration from these examples as they continued their own engagement journey.

1. **Employee Engagement Initiatives**: Angela highlighted examples of employee engagement initiatives that had

yielded impressive results. From wellness programs and team-building activities to leadership development workshops and recognition programs, Angela showcased the diverse range of strategies that had been implemented to boost employee morale and productivity.

2. **Customer Engagement Strategies**: Angela also showcased examples of customer engagement strategies that had captured the hearts and minds of customers around the world. From personalized marketing campaigns and loyalty programs to responsive customer support and community-building initiatives, Angela demonstrated how companies had successfully engaged customers at every touchpoint of their journey.

3. **Integration of Employee and Customer Engagement**: Finally, Angela highlighted examples of companies that had successfully integrated employee and customer engagement initiatives to create a cohesive and impactful experience. These companies recognized that engaged employees were the key to delivering exceptional customer service and building lasting relationships with customers.

As Angela shared these stories of success, the team listened intently, their hearts swelling with pride and inspiration. They marveled at the transformative power of the engagement equation and the impact it had on both employees and customers alike. They felt a renewed sense of purpose and determination, knowing that they had the knowledge and tools to create a workplace and customer experience that truly made a difference.

With a sense of optimism and excitement, Angela and the team set out to apply the lessons learned from their journey, confident that they were on the right path towards building a company where both employee happiness and customer satisfaction thrived. As they embarked on this next chapter of their engagement journey, they knew that the possibilities were endless, and the future was theirs to shape.

Developing an Engagement Roadmap

As Angela continued to inspire the team with real-world examples of successful engagement initiatives, she turned their attention to the practical steps involved in implementing engagement strategies. She emphasized the importance of developing an engagement roadmap, a step-by-step guide to navigating the complexities of engagement and ensuring sustained success.

Step-by-step Guide to Implementing Engagement Strategies

Angela outlined the key components of an engagement roadmap, guiding the team through each stage of the process:

1. **Assessment and Analysis**: Angela emphasized the importance of starting with a thorough assessment of the current state of engagement within the organization. This involved gathering data, soliciting feedback from employees and customers, and conducting a comprehensive analysis of strengths, weaknesses, opportunities, and threats.
2. **Goal Setting**: Angela encouraged the team to set clear and measurable goals for engagement, aligning them with the company's mission, vision, and values. These goals should be specific, achievable, relevant, and time-bound,

providing a roadmap for success and accountability.
3. **Strategy Development**: Angela guided the team through the process of developing engagement strategies that addressed the identified needs and opportunities. This involved brainstorming creative solutions, leveraging best practices and insights from research, and involving stakeholders in the decision-making process.
4. **Implementation and Execution**: Angela stressed the importance of effectively implementing and executing engagement strategies, ensuring that they were communicated clearly, supported by resources, and integrated into daily operations. This involved assigning responsibilities, establishing timelines, and monitoring progress towards goals.

Assessing Progress and Adjusting Strategies

Angela highlighted the importance of regularly assessing progress towards engagement goals and adjusting strategies as needed. This involved gathering feedback from employees and customers, analyzing data and metrics, and evaluating the effectiveness of engagement initiatives.

Angela emphasized the importance of being agile and adaptable in response to changing circumstances, recognizing that engagement was an ongoing journey rather than a destination. She encouraged the team to be open to feedback, willing to experiment with new approaches, and committed to continuous improvement.

As Angela concluded her discussion on developing an engagement roadmap, the team felt empowered and equipped to take action. With a clear understanding of the steps involved and the importance of assessment and adjustment, they set out to develop their own engagement roadmap, confident that they were on the right path towards building a workplace and customer experience that truly thrived.

With a renewed sense of purpose and determination, Angela and the team embarked on the next phase of their engagement journey, ready to apply their knowledge and skills to create positive change. As they worked together to implement their engagement roadmap, they knew that they were making a difference, one step at a time.

Conclusion

As Angela brought the discussion to a close, she guided the team through a reflective recap of their journey towards achieving balance and success in engagement. With a sense of pride and accomplishment, she emphasized the importance of balancing employee happiness and customer satisfaction, recognizing that both were essential ingredients for sustained success.

Recap of Key Insights

Angela revisited the key insights and lessons learned from their exploration of the engagement equation:

1. **Understanding Engagement**: Angela emphasized the importance of understanding the multifaceted nature of engagement, recognizing that it encompassed both employee happiness and customer satisfaction.
2. **Developing Strategies**: Angela guided the team through the process of developing effective engagement strategies,

emphasizing the importance of alignment with company values, cultural sensitivity, and continuous improvement.
3. **Implementing the Roadmap**: Angela outlined the steps involved in implementing an engagement roadmap, from assessment and analysis to goal setting, strategy development, and execution. She highlighted the importance of regular assessment and adjustment to ensure sustained success.

Final Thoughts on Balancing Employee Happiness and Customer Satisfaction

As Angela concluded her discussion, she shared her final thoughts on the importance of balancing employee happiness and customer satisfaction:

"Throughout our journey, we've seen firsthand the transformative power of engagement in driving both employee and customer outcomes. By prioritizing the well-being of our employees and fostering meaningful connections with our customers, we've not only achieved balance but also unlocked new levels of success and growth.

As we move forward, let us remember that engagement is not just a business strategy but a way of life. It's about creating a workplace and customer experience where people feel valued, respected, and empowered to make a difference. By embracing the principles of the engagement equation, we can create a world where both employees and customers thrive, and where success knows no bounds."

With a renewed sense of purpose and determination, Angela and the team embraced the challenge of balancing employee happiness and customer satisfaction, confident that they were on the right path towards building a brighter future for themselves and their company. As they reflected on their journey, they knew that the engagement equation would continue to guide them in their quest for success, ensuring that they never lost sight of what truly mattered: people.

About the Author

Goodson Mumba is a multifaceted individual known for his diverse expertise and prolific contributions across various fields. As an infopreneur, thought leader, and spiritual leader, he has inspired countless individuals through his insightful teachings and impactful writings. Mumba is also an accomplished author, with several notable works to his name, including "Understanding Corporate Worship," "The Years I Spent in a Week," "Management By Harmony," "The CEO's Diary," "Change to Change" and "Creative Thinking for results" His literary works span topics ranging from business management to personal development and spirituality, reflecting his broad range of interests and insights.

With a Master of Business Leadership (MBL) and a Bachelor of Arts in Theology (BTh), Mumba brings a unique blend of business acumen and spiritual wisdom to his work. His educational background is further enriched by a Group Diploma in Management Studies, providing him with a solid foundation in organizational dynamics and leadership principles. Additionally, Mumba holds diplomas in Education Psychology,

Leadership and Management Styles, Organizational Behaviour, Financial Accounting, Economic Growth and Development, and Project Management, showcasing his commitment to continuous learning and professional development.

Mumba's expertise extends beyond traditional academic disciplines, encompassing areas such as Neuro-Linguistic Programming (NLP) and Positive Psychology. His diverse skill set is complemented by a range of certifications, including Creative Problem Solving and Decision Making, Life Coaching Fundamentals and Techniques, Professional Life Coaching, and Performance Management System Design. These certifications reflect Mumba's dedication to equipping himself with the tools and knowledge necessary to empower others and drive positive change.

As an author, Mumba's writings reflect his deep understanding of human nature, organizational dynamics, and spiritual principles. His works offer practical insights, actionable strategies, and inspirational guidance for individuals seeking personal growth, professional success, and spiritual fulfillment. Mumba's holistic approach to life and leadership resonates with readers worldwide, making him a respected figure in both the business and spiritual communities.

Overall, Goodson Mumba's diverse background, extensive knowledge, and profound insights make him a sought-after speaker, mentor, and author. His commitment to excellence, lifelong learning, and service to others continues to inspire individuals to unlock their full potential and lead lives of purpose and significance.

Goodson Mumba is renowned for initiating the concept of Management by Harmony, revolutionizing traditional management practices with a focus on balanced and holistic approaches. He has authored two influential books on this subject: "Introduction to Management by Harmony" and its sequel, "Management by Harmony."

Mumba's work has significantly impacted the field, offering innovative strategies for fostering organizational harmony and efficiency. His contributions continue to shape contemporary management theories and practices.

www.ingramcontent.com/pod-product-compliance
Lightning Source LLC
Chambersburg PA
CBHW071834210526
45479CB00001B/137